# I Sing, Does that Mean I Am Happy …

AUTUMN W. FISHER

WESTBOW®
PRESS
A DIVISION OF THOMAS NELSON
& ZONDERVAN

WestBow Press books may be ordered through booksellers or by contacting:

WestBow Press
A Division of Thomas Nelson & Zondervan
1663 Liberty Drive
Bloomington, IN 47403
www.westbowpress.com
1 (866) 928-1240

ISBN: 978-1-4908-2404-8 (sc)
ISBN: 978-1-4908-2405-5 (e)

Library of Congress Control Number: 2014901566
Printed in the United States of America.

WestBow Press rev. date: 01/23/2014

# CONTENTS

# THIS BOOK IS DEDICATED TO:

All the people that caused me a good deal of hurt and such a horrendous unimaginable beginning, without whom I probably would never have perceived the intense need for such a book. Making this book a genuine asset to fellow sufferers along with those who want to know what to watch out for to keep this from happening to you or anyone you know, and to those wanting to learn from others whose tragic recounts betters their understanding in how they can truly be a help to the hurting.

And to my wonderful husband who has stood by me through the writing of this book having to hear a multitude of horrible unfathomable accounts of my earlier life, giving me comfort as well as support, I am truly blessed!

Finally, to my Heavenly Father, His son Jesus, and the Holy Spirit; without the love and care they have given and shown me throughout my whole life thus far I would not have made it. They have kept me safe from death, hate and bitterness, I owe them my talents, my time, my gratitude, but most of all, I owe them the very breath they gave me!

# INTRODUCTION

When I was a Junior in high school my English class teacher gave the class a writing assignment. We were to write a paragraph or two, telling a little bit about ourselves. I, like the rest of my class, wrote as we were instructed. After a good while she began laying out our writing schedule as it would be expected from that day forward, until the end of our class year. She told us that we would be expected to write in our journals every class day upon arrival, we would be given fifteen to twenty minutes to do so. We could write about anything, just write something.

WOW, I thought, this is right up my alley. I inherited a love for writing from my father's side of the family. I started writing when I was very young, around six or seven years of age. I grew up hearing my grandmother's poetry and stories, they were so fascinating to me. I would sit at her feet begging to hear more. My father, her son, was talented in this area as well as being able to sing and play several musical instruments. I suppose then, that it would seem reasonable that at least one of my father's six children would inherit this gift as well, that would be me.

Days and weeks passed, one season turning to another; as did the pages of writings in my journal. I wrote about many things, and in various genre's, mostly poetry. It made me very happy to have been given a time to do what I thoroughly enjoy doing, it gave me an avenue to release a lot of feelings that were pinned up inside of me. I could, and have, on many occasions wrote for hours and still not be ready to quit.

Then one day after our allotted time of writing, much to our surprise, the teacher collected our journals. I was suddenly in a panic, I never thought that these would be read. She rummaged through them halting as she came to mine, I knew it was mine because of the color, it was the only bright yellow one in the room, everybody knew it was mine. She held it, flipping to what I had just written, she was reading it to herself. After, what seemed like eternity, she looked up and straight at me, I couldn't imagine what she was going to say or do with it. I shrank in my seat hoping to disappear.

"You are such a happy girl, you laugh and sing all the time........how can you write these horribly sad things? There is so much violence, blood, and despair; I don't understand this........."

Oh, wow! I was so embarrassed, my face was burning hot, I knew that it was very red. What was I to say?! I was stunned. I sat motionless, I couldn't move if I wanted to. Everyone was still staring at me.

"Well, I am not a happy person", I quietly stated.

She laughed as she said, "RIGHT!"

Now, the whole room was filled with boisterous laughter as if I had just told an extremely funny joke. I guess to them, I had.

# THE VIOLATION

## Chapter I

Sharing bits and pieces of our lives almost always brings a smile to all those that hear them, but there are those portions that we want to keep hidden deep inside, those pieces of our lives that would be of no benefit to anyone; so, there is no reason to bring them up....or is there?

Let's step back a moment and re-examine our past, going back to a time in our early childhood days, a time when things were so simple. We can see ourselves with others, we're laughing, smiling, running and playing, the neighborhood children gathered at your house, or your cousins and/or other family members seemed to always be there; you all were having so much fun, not a care in the world. In fact, if asked, we would say that these were the "best times" of our lives. Having essentially, no responsibilities. It never occurred to us that this was temporary. We never imagined that they would ever change, nor that these people would come and go, in and out of our lives, throughout our lifetime. Life was good.

Now, let's remember a time in your past that wasn't so happy. What happened to change your happy to sad? Being that this is a memory from your childhood; had you simply tripped and fell? Or, were you learning to ride your first bike and that person you trusted to hang on, let go, and then you fell? The possibilities are endless. Maybe you can't quite remember every hurt or reason for it, but you do recall some sort of sadness. You can remember hurts of all types from skinned knees and elbows to your first broken heart, even though these are typical for everyone when you experienced each one, they were your wounds and hurts. Some you get over pretty quickly, while others cause you a great deal of pain, then there are those happenings that scar you physically, emotionally, and even spiritually. These scars in whichever form they are categorized can be lifelong and debilitating if allowed to remain.

Having brought these memories from your past to your present, you can see that, even though, they are pretty common incidences, they brought with them a remembrance of that pain that is all too predictable. I mean, falling will almost always bring some measure of pain with it, and not only is it painful to the person who fell, it causes a great deal of discomfort or even some measure of hurt to the observer, sometimes more. If you are a parent, grandparent or someone who is in the childcare business, then you understand what I mean, when you see a child that is falling you are already cringing before they have even hit the thing they are falling toward. You can almost feel that impending pain. There are just as many reasons or actions that cause us pain and sadness, as there are to us being happy. And knowing that there are numerous examples of these things, or times that can, and do, cause real pain; we can't stop them all from happening. The elders in our lives say, "It's normal, nearly everyone in the world experiences them sometime or another in their lives, many are worse than others. And, it is almost a guarantee that there are more to come until we draw our last breath".

So, with that being said; this is normal and is just a phase or part of our maturation stages, we begin to deal with these hurts ourselves; some people do better than others. And there are many explanations as to why: some, grow up in stable environments where the "family takes care of its own". Bringing a sense of confidence, knowing they are not alone, someone is there to help them through their hurts and/or problems. Then, there are those who never know the comfort of a traditional home and family, they have basically raised themselves and/or their siblings, or maybe they had to take care of the person(s) that should have been taking care of them, you see this a lot with drug and alcohol abusers, with that comes feelings of sadness and most always a degree of resentment. And then, there are those who are brought up with Christian values and morals that are to equip them for whatever life brings. There is stability in having roots in Christianity, we know that we are not alone and we can go to the Father for help anytime anywhere.

So, let me ask you, "Were you one of the fortunate, that grew up in a small mid western town, like I did? Where everybody knew everybody else, and come Sunday morning you were up early and getting ready for church. You wore your best clothes (church clothes), and was very proud to do so?"

Church was such a perfect place, where you felt special. You would see all of your family and friends greeting you, as well as each other, with smiles and open arms, like everyone was so thrilled to see you, even if you'd only just seen them the evening before. You felt a sense of peace and contentment, you felt loved, like you belonged, it was a "safe house" because God was there! Everyone knew each other and helped each other in any way they could. It didn't matter much that everyone seemed to know your business. Then one day, something happened that changed your life forever, like it did mine. Someone you trusted or you should have been able to trust, crossed a line, using their position/authority over you to take advantage of your trust/innocence. Their reckless disregard for you and your happiness, not to mention your dignity, showed that they cared little for how this was going to effect you your whole life, but more than anything, they have wrecked your "safe place (house)"!

The violation is hideous and mind-numbing by itself, but it brings with it some ugly, disturbing, life altering attachments, such as; shock, insecurity, sadness, fear, negativity, disgust, a feeling of self loathing, feeling so filthy you can't scrub yourself clean enough, bitterness, and hatred; of course, this is in nowise a complete list and not everyone suffers with all or even half of these listed. Then, there are those who carry a lot of these attachments throughout their entire life causing even more havoc with themselves and anyone else they come across in their lifetime, such as, mild forms of sickness that seem like pretty common things like colds or fatigue to pretty severe bouts that cause them to be in and out of mental institutions. The relationships they form throughout the years following are tainted with emotional upheavals, which, in turn drives the very people they need, away. There really isn't a clear cut method or study to recognizing or detecting them all. They embed themselves deep within, only to reappear in other forms, such as; unexplainable outbursts, fighting, insecurity, obsessions etc......., leaving the unsuspecting family, friends, and co-workers to wonder; "what has happened...... or I don't know why they are acting like this", to "they sure have changed.....". They have no idea that this "change" is due to such a hideous crime.

Sometimes, it's sad to say, the violated has become the violator, reclaiming a sense of "power" that had been taken from them when they were the victim. This is not to say that they are committing the same crime, certainly not; but, it is also not saying that they're not. Some feel a sense of "entitlement" because this happened to them, therefore......... It is also believed by many that anyone, if not all, of the abused will themselves become abusers. I have known many people on all three sides: 1. the victims 2. the perpetrator 3. the person who is neither of the other two, but have an opinion just the same. You can find that all statements are true, it has everything to do with: 1. who they are on the inside and how they see themselves. 2.the people and/or thoughts they surround themselves with. 3.And .......do they have a personal connection with God. In all my readings thus far I have concluded that the writings of a very well known book are all true, keep our minds free from revenge, anger, hate, bitterness, and all manner of evil, instead focus on good things, rejoice in the LORD always, love your neighbor as God has loved us and the church, turn from our wicked ways, seek His face and His will, He will never leave us nor turn His back on us if we are sincerely and truly living for Him. We are the ones who do the turning and walking away.

Yet, there are a great number of the violated that just want to get past this ugly hurtful time in their life. They are usually so head strong to do so, that they become almost obsessed with a job or studies, or almost anything that gets them as far away from their past and the ever looming memories as they can get. Though, to the persons around them, they appear to be dedicated to whatever road in life they've chosen. They almost feel a bit threatened or inadequate when working with these people, like they care more for their job or position than they do about them, causing an invisible rift between them. There is nothing wrong with being passionate about something, nor wanting to be the best that you can be, it is a problem when it truly has become an obsession. It is better to deal with the underlying reasons, for the obsession rather than continuing down a road that always has trouble just around the bend. One should rather focus on the good things, rejoicing in the LORD always.

People that have never had this happen to them or anyone else they know, may have a hard time understanding the things that I have mentioned. It is not to say that, because they have not had any confrontation with such matters, it isn't true or doesn't happen or exist. Them being so sheltered from the realities of this crime would keep them in a "Life is grand, nothing bad ever happens" state. I do say, "GREAT!" I'm happy for them, but the chances of this being true is very unlikely. Don't suppose for one minute that I'm questioning their honesty, if they truly believe that this crime is far removed from them and their circle of friends or even their family, I believe that they're far too busy with, "themselves", to notice the subtle hints or warning signs. Leaving that suffering person with one less help, and wondering," why can't they see that I'm in trouble and desperately need them?"

I have noticed that there are a certain number of people that only show their care and concern at certain times or seasons of the year, feeling they have done "their" part taking away any guilt that might have dusted their clothes Sunday morning. They walk with their breasts/chests puffed out and their heads held high, all pressed and pleated, even a great and notable flood couldn't cover their airways. So, they do NO one any good, mostly not themselves. When tragedy trikes their circle; their family, friends, neighbors and public people they hold dear they are usually the first to fold. The lack of control will almost drive them insane. We rarely see this because they have their thoughts so far removed from "reality" they'll hardly recognize a person in trouble or need.

I am just as surprised at how many people DO know about the abuse happening, no matter how awful, but yet choose to ignore it so that they don't have to deal with it. Even in my own life and the violations I endured/survived, there are people that were near to me in every way including proximity that still say to this day they never knew, they claim that they've blocked out portions of their lives. While this may help them move on with their heads in the sand, it helps no one! I believe that they will be held accountable for it; it is written also that anyone that knows to do right but doesn't do it, is committing a wrong/sin.

You may be one of these abused people that seem to be just going through the motions of living, trying to appear okay on the outside but, on the inside your heart is broken, you would rather stay in a room shut off from the rest of the world, and hope you are not bothered until the end of time; I want you to know and always remember: upon reading these words you will no longer be "the victim or the violated" you are "VICTORIOUS!" Your life may have been a mess all along, but from here on out you'll have someone helping you and caring for your every concern.

And if you are the violator, you are not reading this by chance or by accident; this is your opportunity to change "repent". You can be forgiven! Don't approach your victims and feel they are going to feel such great joy and decide to wipe it out as if it never happened, but your forgiveness comes from God Himself. He will and can change you, He can make you whiter than snow, and it will be as if you'd never sinned or committed this wrong. You have to be truly sorry, God knows our hearts and intentions. The person(s) that have suffered because of your action(s) will have to ask for help getting over their wounds, hurts, and sufferings. God will help them heal inwardly and outwardly, as well as bring them into the full reality of true forgiveness.

And finally, if you are one of the persons I described having your mind so far out of what is going on around you, please stop! Take a good look around........are there hurting, homeless, abused and neglected people within your reach? Repent "change" and begin today to help where and when you can, the more you help the more your focus will adjust to right things. You aren't reading this just by chance, you are being given ANOTHER chance to change!

tormented night and day with these questions. They will probably remain unanswered because you are too fearful to voice them to others, opening up that seething pit, that would cause them to think ill of you. Knowing that this, fear almost assuredly keeps the victim quiet, thus allowing the crime to go unpunished.

Finding yourself in this seemingly, "no win" situation, you of course, would be frightened and very confused; not only do you have the aforementioned questions running through your mind, you have to deal with keeping yourself and everything else in check, to maintain an outwaaard sense of normalcy. People you know and thought were "on your side" turn out to be strangers, somehow blaming you for the unGodly acts of another. Like it is somehow your fault that this person couldn't control themselves nor their actions causing so much saddness, pain, and grief.

It may be baffling to you, the unharmed, as well, to hear a person say that they have to keep quiet and seem normal, but then say; "Why can't they see?" (meaning: others that could help) You wonder why the hurting wouldn't want to run and tell the nearest available person.

I know in my experience, I was told if I didn't do what was expected or if I said anything to anyone, I would be told on for something I hadn't done; but being just 3-4 years of age that would be bad as far as I was concerned then. I can also remember an ocassion where I was tied up in the presence of other children and at least one other adult, and then taken to a bridge that was way out in the country, it was so dark and cold out. I was very afraid. I was then told that I was going to be thrown from that bridge and even though I was very young, I realized, that I was going to die that night and no one would even know it, no one outside of these people. I noticed that as I grew older the threats were more severe to keep the unknow too scary to even think about dealing with. I have no idea in what way the memory of the bridge incident affected me, but you can believe that it did!

I was not allowed to stay at anyone's house, go to school functions, or have a job outside away from these people's sight. Many times I would be beaten just to solidify my compliance to expected silence, and on more than a few ocassions, my caretaker would have her suspicions about me doing various wrong doings. Which were, of course, untrue, but that didn't keep her from taking a 3" wide x 1/2" thick leather strap to me, wherever it hit was fine with her, wether it was my face or my legs she didn't care, the hanger part of the strap came loose and struck me repeatedly. I am not saying that the regular beatings I received were the only forms of abuse I suffered, nor were they the worst! I was mocked when I cried and pleaded for them to stop, they seemed to enjoy my pain; the more I hurt, the happier they became. So, early on, I decided; they would never see me cry again, nor would I show any emotions happy or sad, I did not cry, smile, or laugh when I was around them. I had no joy only heartach. I, at a very tender age, had earned the nickname,"Old Stone Cold Heart".

If you have never dealt with anything like this you are probably finding it a little hard to believe, that in this day and age of technology, and the outrageous displays of "freedom of speech", and our fast paced lives; how could this be kept in secret? It's easier than one might think. You have seen or heard of people in the news all the time that have done some horrible things to their loved ones and when family, friends and neighbors are interviewed you hear, more times than not, "They were so loving with each other, they were so happy, and such a quiet family. Do not let the smiles and light laughter lull you into missing really big cues, and/or signs of change. No matter the age or gender, social status, political title, organization membership, or even religious affiliation, anyone could be an abuser, that person you would probably never suspect, the most likable, overly friendly, and seems to have "it all together" just may have a secret, a skeleton in their closet. And most assuredly, anyone can be a victim. Someone who has fallen prey to someone who has become a social deviant. We can't imagine how often someone sits in our company or crosses our path, for one reason or another, that is hurting on the inside, hoping someone would find out and come to their rescue. And because it is so difficult to know what to look for, they go away in the same helpless, hopeless and tormented condition as when we first encountered them. How sick would we be to find out those statistics, God forgive us and help us to re-examine our encounters, realizing that these are opportunities for us to help those who are in great need, and in helping them we might begin to "turn the tide", making this a better, safer place to live.

Let's turn our focus, for just a bit, to a number of the attachments that are associated with various types and varying degrees of abuse. There is an embarrassment that goes along with being abused, which is also a hard to understand fact. The abuser in this case, really doesn't have to do much to keep the offense(s) from being exposed, because that is the last thing the victim wants; letting everyone in on their deepest darkest secret, that disgusting thing that causes them so much torment; that thing that is eating them alive from the inside out. Sharing such an awful fact about themselves, is too much. They somehow feel responsible. We, of course, know that this is far from the truth. One of the reasons they feel embarrassed is the stigma that goes along with it, from the point of discovery on; no matter how it comes to light, that abused person suffers, not only the lasting effects of the acts themselves, but wherever they go between the whispers and finger pointing, they are marked for what has been done to them, instead of their true accomplishments and aspirations they have for their life.

The abused also has this sense of responsibility that they, somehow, have to keep quiet to protect those realitives, business partners, organizations, neighbors, and/or their church family from finding out just how bad this person really is. They are just trying to survive in most cases.

A lot of the violated feel shame and self-reproach, a filthiness that; no matter how hard they try, they can't wash away. They hate themselves and their life, wishing they could just die, and sadly, they do most times attempt to take their own life, some are successful. They're disgusted with themselves. Thinking if they were somehow better or had made other choices this wouldn't be happening. They see no other way out or way to handle their, "mountain".

I know of a young man, 18, who had been in an abusive situation he was so distraught and embarrassed that he'd become a victim because he perceived that he was, "still in complete control". He tried to confront his abuser the only way he knew how; upon realizing the exact opposite was true; he had no contol over the other person and what he had suffered at that persons words/hands, he made a verbal threat where he threatened to end his own life. He was trying to exact an acknowledgment of what this person had done to him, in the presence of witnesses. He was wanting the perpetrator to show remorse for what he had done to him. The man claimed his innocence thereby making a public joke of this young man, of course the "witnesses" left with the perpetrator, laughing as they exited. Having suffered, yet again, at the hands of this man, he left to fulfill his earlier threat. Sadly, he carried it through. Afterward, at his funeral it could be heard by many, that if they had just known how serious he was they would have spoken with him......REALLY?! It has been a few years now, and I think of this horrible tragedy it causes me to speak out all the more.

The biggest red flag, for a possible sign that one is being abused, that I have witnessed, is when you encounter a miniature adult. A child who seems wiser and more advanced in knowledge than most adults. Knowing things that really should not be known for someone their age. This is not usually the ones who mimic their parents or other important persons in the childs life. Now, that's not to say that every child that is well knowledged or seems adult like, is a victim of abuse, but it does warrant some attention. I find myself watching and listening for possible red flags and clues that something might be wrong, but, in the same respect; not every child is being abused, nor every adult a victim of a bad childhood, or a potential criminal. There really are "real" happy, well adjusted, and healthy families out there!

Again, this is in no wise, the complete listings of the full extent of damage, abuse brings about or causes, in a single individual. Imagine, if you will, what it must sound like to our God to hear all of the crys, prayers, and groanings from HIS hurting children, ALL at the same time......CONTINUOUSLY !!!!! And yet, the one sitting right next to the one drowning in the depths of despair, hears nothing, sees nothing, and so.......does nothing!

I challenge each person reading this book or just these few words to look around, right there where you're at! In your own homes, neighborhood, church etc............, watch for little signs or red flags, then help those individuals. It's not an easy thing, it can be frightening to step up and do the right thing, but just think if you don't help what will happen to that person in the next minute, hours, days, or even years? So what if you sound crazy, these prisoners of abuse are counting on our help! Don't stop if you truly believe something isn't right, go with your gut, God gave us an intuition for a reason, but we usually stifle it or chalk it up to something else. Meanwhile, the secrecy is successful.

So, please pray and let God lead you, and don't be afraid to ask questions and be aware of your neighbors who should be around their place, as well as, knowing who shouldn't be. Make sure to communicate with your family, friends, and neighbors. Be a good listener, a lot of bad things can be curbed or settled by letting them speak it out, it might be something as simple as them feeling overlooked or insignificant. Unfortunatly, that isn't true with all circumstances sometimes it is just as simple as, "the wrong place at the wrong time". Don't ever fall into believing that God did this, not for any reason!!! He did NOT!!!

# WHO CAN I TELL OR TRUST?

## Chapter III

All throughout our lives we develop friendships and have connections and relationships of various types. In the beginning of each, we form the opinion as to whether or not we can trust these persons to have our back. Even as children we choose our "best friend(s)", and as the days, weeks, months, and years fly by, many will be replaced. There will be a select few that come and go only to return again; and an even fewer number will be with you the whole way.

There, from these groups, are those that you can trust more than others. Some, you can only share little insignificant things with, no matter how many years you know them, it is a shallow friendship, not much past acquaintance. Others, you can share a little bit more, but still nothing crucial, or life altering. It's not that they are wanting to betray your trust or get on your bad side, they either can't keep things confidential or they're needing some sort of validation to fit in with another potential friend. Which is sad really, because these people find themselves on the outs with others pretty often. Their life, in general, is usually filled with "DRAMA". They seem to almost thrive on it, but no matter tried and true good or bad, they are your friend.

What can we say attracts one person to another; would it be their physical appearance, their personality, or their overall mannerisms? I don't believe that it is ever one clear attribute, but rather, two or more. It could be a sincere admiration for an independent air or as simple as proximity, whether it be true physical locale or by being relatives, or you recognize a similar character trait and/or problem area. Whatever it is, we join ourselves to them and them to us, spending the rest of our days entangled in and out of the webs, troubles, and issues of life. That's not to say, that there were not peaceful and fun times along the way, because there are many shared moments throughout the years. I'm positive that given a moment to think back, any one of us could recall a memory that we hold dear and that when remembered would bring a smile.

Having made these choices as to whom you are or are not going to be friends with, you deal with the pangs and joys of life. Then, on one unsuspecting day, you suffer at the hands of another. You want, and so desperately need to tell someone. You're not exactly sure what you're wanting them to do, even though you, of course, want the person(s) caught and the wrongful act(s) to stop. You're not actually wanting them to do the telling, nor judge the person(s) or the situation. Mostly you are wanting a shoulder to cry on and/or them to just be a good listener. And depending on the circumstance(s), they may be called upon, by you, to give some simple answers or suggestions ie.; "What should I do? If this was you, what would you do? Or Can you believe this person is capable of doing this?" It is reasonable for them to assume you'll practice confidentiality, and until proven to be false, they expect you to believe them. And as heart wrenching as all of this can be it is worth your time and patience, these people need help because in most cases have no idea what to do, let alone where to go, so giving them an ear or shoulder is of great importance to them.

I have experienced, more times than I care to remember or want to waste time calculating, trying to let someone know that I needed help, only to have them turn back and side with the perpetrator. I can't express enough, just how damaging this can be to a victim. And depending on how many times a person has this done to them, it's like being victimized over and over again. Each time I had carefully scoped out and closely observed each individual long before trying to approach them for help. I wasn't wanting to repeat the same mistakes as I had before; thinking that the ones I had chosen as my place of refuge, would help me because it was the right thing to do. I am appalled at how many had actually felt a sense of loyalty toward the person(s) who had committed these heinous crimes. It, to me was not only hurtful but insulting. They hadn't, in most cases, decided that it was untrue, but; it was as if they had said to me, "okay, we don't deny that this has/is happening, but they have been my friend for years, they've never done anything to me." I have actually had that said, as well as, "it can't be that bad". "What do you want me to do about it !!! Oh, this can't be true." Once in my very early years I had had a person that I trusted enough to tell ask me things in such a manner and verbage I couldn't understand any of what she said. The words were none I'd ever heard. The only reason I knew that they were questions was by the look on her face and the fact that she paused waiting for me to respond.

Having to deal with these very difficult and trying attempts, seeing that they'd been nothing but futile; to get my life restored to a "normal" socially acceptable state, it left me a bit skittish. I had resolved myself to believing, that I was trapped in this horrible nightmare, with no way out and no one to come to my rescue! I had even sought help from a couple of children my age but it wasn't long before I realized, by the look on their faces, they were shocked and couldn't believe it. I hadn't hardly got started telling them my plight when, after their response, I decided they were of no help to me, I went on about my way.............. saddened even deeper and more alone. I dreaded each day. I would sit alone on the embankment alongside the road watching the sun set, I longed to be "normal" like everyone else. Many times while I sat there certain ones would come to me, but only to give a quick salute or cheery word, then be on their way hoping not to get too involved in my apparent struggles that would keep them from their course, whether it be fun or work.

I was spoken of as the, "odd child", because of my sadness and preference of solitude. I wasn't wanting to be this way it just happened. I longed to be really happy, I tried to overlook the bad things that were going on in my life, but it was too much, sorrow and pain seemed to be my constant companions. I laughed all the time, you can ask anyone that knows me and they will testify to that, even to this day,but I was only laughing on the outside and crying on the inside.

Upon reading this and the above statements, you're probably thinking that telling or trying to get help, or even, just trying to get someone to listen; is impossible. That isn't the thoughts or impression I want you to glean from this writing. You should speak out! Never keep abuse a secret, it doesn't matter what you've been threatened with or how many people you have to trust or confide in, ABUSE IS

NEVER OKAY!!!! It doesn't matter who believes you or not, just keep telling until someone listens and the abuse stops! Over and over we hear these words, but how often have they been pushed aside only to become settled in believing, "this is it......my life.........there's a reason for everything", but it isn't if we never give up! God will make a way where there seems to be no way, we can't give up or admit defeat.

I do have to include this in this chapter, because I want to further open your eyes and raise the awareness to the fact that; not all victims are fortunate enough to escape or survive without using some measure of witty opportunism. Taking mental notes of names, places, and/ or quirks of the captor ; and their areas of vulnerability. By paying close attention to these facts, even the smallest tidbit would prove most valuable in getting free, especially in making sure that your abuser is apprehended. Never believe the lies; that you are helpless, and that no one cares, you are all alone. This is simply not true!!!

Sometimes, as with myself, the victim has had to devise a plan to free themselves. Finding that there really isn't any other way to escape their torment. I had chosen to refuse compliance, knowing that it would most likely lead to a fight for my life. I, like I had anticipated, faced my "giant". I was, at that moment, ready and willing to lay my very last breath on the line before that person would ever hurt me again! I engaged in the physical battle of my life, I was willing to die at that point, to be free. The actual attack came when I was completely unaware, I was asleep, I believed that I was safe. I engaged in battle with someone that was two and a half times heavier than myself, nearly two foot taller, and was at least twenty years older. It felt like, at first, this was an impossible feat of endurance. Then, just when I felt I was about to lose, I, in an instant knew, I would not suffer much longer. I am not certain how many minutes the fight lasted, to me, it seemed like an eternity. I did win, and from that day to this, that person has never physically abused me again.

I, also wish I could say that this was my only occasion of being violated, woefully, it wasn't. I, although only describing an overview of the abuse I had received, had intentionally held back the detailed descriptions as to not focus explicitly on them, thereby taking away from my main objective for this book. So, to make it very clear; this particular portion or descriptions I have given, are in nowise the only injuries, hurts (physical/mental), woes or abuse (verbal/physical/mental) I have received. And there was by no means, one perpetrator! BUT,praise God! I am a survivor! You are too! Let God be God!

I realize there are many who will read this and not believe a word of it, I can't help that. I am thankful that they have never had this happen to them. I am reaching out, with this book, to all of those who have, or will be going through like situations. I wish it were true, that this isn't real, or doesn't happen, all people; past, present, and future, are happy/safe and good. But, the sad fact is; "bad" has happened, is happening, and will continue in varying degrees until the end.

# WHAT WILL HAPPEN IF I TELL?

## Chapter IV

Having already addressed the topic of whom you could trust we'll continue to our next troublesome issue, "What will happen if I tell?" that is a very big question and greater concern. The person(s) holding you captive in this torment, either by physical restraints or mentally, by threatening the health or safety of yourself and/or friends and family keep you in a continual state of fear. Just the mere mention of impending doom on someone so dear to you as your closest friend or family member, you feel you must cooperate with this fiend.

When a younger child is being threatened, the captor usually doesn't have to be too detailed or too devious, but if the age of the victim is older, then, the threat has to be harsher something so unthinkable their compliance is a certainty. Imposing such horrendous visions of described and promised hurt will be with them for many years even after their escape, return, or release. You would probably be astonished to learn just how big the numbers are of the people who seek therapy, for one reason or another, for things pertaining to abuse in some form sometime in their life. Don't think for one moment that all abuse is reported, or that you hear about all cases that are publicized, if you did it would be too overwhelming.

I recall in the early years of my life, I was somewhere around two or three years of age, I was already hurting and afraid, I had no thoughts of this being wrong or right because I was so little when my nightmare began; I just knew that it was not what I wanted! I still to this day, have no idea why, after all of my screaming and crying, no one came to help me! Where was my family, friends, or... the neighbors?!!! By my sixth year. I was told that, if I yelled or gave them any trouble, not only would I receive a beating which left big purplish red welts on my body, it would be know that I had done...( It changed many times as to what I would be falsely accused of doing. The people in charge of me, were equally as cruel as this person, so, I didn't want any further confrontations with them.). I had resigned myself to the fact that this was my life. I had believed that this was the way it was, every child had this happening to them... right?

It wasn't until I was older that I learned, that this was called;"abuse" ( to hurt or injure by maltreatment, misuse), and it doesn't happen to everyone, and you should get help. From where? I realized early on, of there being an ever present danger of the people that I run to for help; getting hurt themselves. OR, what if; they don't believe me for one reason or another, ie; my age, people tend to chalk all stories from youngsters up to, just that....stories. Another reason for people's supposed disbelief is the person(s) in question themselves and the people they know, as well as the clubs, groups and/or organizations they belong to. And too, unlike today, various crimes were not discussed. Back when I was born, in the sixties, a lot of things were "taboo", of course, it didn't mean it didn't happen; it just wasn't talked about. So, I, had reconciled to figuring it out myself. I, at that age, had suffered varied forms of abuse, and by that time the threat was presented as a "promise", but, as I have already stated, I suffered!!!

So, I decided that the promised hurt that would come as a result of my telling, could not ever compare to what I had already endured! I knew there was no other acceptable option. After something so horrid and inexplicably severe; what could they do that could ever be worse?

I know that after the above statement one would think that I've ruled out being killed by the abuser, I had not... I was well aware of that ever present reality but at that time I didn't care. I am sharing what I went through and what I was thinking, for me, and that moment, that is the only conclusion I could see. Yes, sadly, there are times, far too many, when someone is killed, I still say.... TELL!!! That is the only way to get it to stop!!!

I was, I suppose, a little brainwashed into believing that if I told, the people that I told it to, would be angry with me. Because of my lack of trust issues I sure didn't need or want anymore negativity. I sought out other ways of trying to cope with my dilemma.

I have recently heard of a case where a baby was taken while the father was at work, he came home to find the sitter was gone and so was his infant son. He searched and called everywhere he could think of and yet, could not find his son. The police exhausted their resources, as the days, weeks, and months slowly turned into years many gave up hope but not the grieving father, he hired private investigators. Sadly, they too, followed what few leads they had to go on turning up with nothing. Then, one day out of the blue thirteen years later the father's phone rang; the voice he heard on the other end spoke the very words he'd wanted to hear so long ago, and many times since the beginning of his nightmare. The person calling was a sheriff from seven states away and he said that the man's son has been found. The father got off work and drove the nineteen hours to get his now fourteen year old boy. The child had been taken by his grand mother, she was his sitter. She, of course, was arrested and placed in jail awaiting her fate.

Now, you may have various questions: Why was it so hard to trace this baby when the authorities already knew who the perpetrator was? Why had it taken fourteen years to apprehend her with today's technology? Why had she taken him in the first place? Where is his mother? We will probably never know the answer to every one, but he's back with his father, so, all is well..........

Or is it? I have run this over in my head and cannot see a "happily ever after" ending. How will these two relate? I mean, the boy never knew his dad because he never knew that he was stolen until the day he was removed from his school room by a sheriff from a place he'd never been. He knows the only family he's ever known has been arrested and put behind bars. In all these years did the father start another family, are there other children this boy will have to get used to? When he interacted with other children through the years what was going through his mind about his family, or lack thereof? During the entire ordeal what was this woman thinking, had she abused him in any other way, well, besides the initial crime of kidnapping?

God can do anything, especially those things that we deem impossible. He can take this awful tragic story and turn it into one of the greatest recovery stories we've ever heard, but it has to be with God, if He is left out or not even considered then the chances of this working out are next to impossible.

Let's examine a little closer what is happening with the boy. He was an infant when this nightmare began, as he aged and went through the natural phases and stages everyone goes through ie; rolling over, crawling, feeding himself, talking, walking etc........., loving the only person he knew (the grand mother who stole him ); how then can he ever believe this unbelievable tale as he watches it unfold right before him and in every public forum? Will he feel a certain loyalty toward this grand mother and thereby resent his true father for causing his present upheaval? He will undoubtedly harbor a deep seeded resentment and bitterness toward his father, his father may have him in the physical, but she has him in the heart. I am not trying to bring you down but these are the facts, it is sad and happens every day!

This poor father has missed out on so much that most people take for granted, all of the child's firsts; he will want and try so desperately to recapture, which we know won't work because we can't turn back time. We will probably hear where this young man took a terrible turn in his life after this, of course we pray not, but unless God is in the equation it will happen. Am I saying then, that one should give up the search for missing children knowing this painful but true fact........no, I'm not! God, like I said, can / will do the impossible because with Him ALL things are possible! Look, look and keep looking! Never give up the hope of finding them.

Now, on to you, as with anything there are always certain risks involved, you have to consider the alternative. Are you certain that the situation you are in or that you know of truly an abusive one? Can you say that the present condition you find yourself in is one totally contrary to God's plan? These two questions may seem the same in nature, but are instead very different. The first one is asking if the things in your everyday life, whether in a relationship or not, are abusive, meaning; the people you are around or have to deal with in a daily manner. Just because someone's disrespectful disposition is something to be avoided, doesn't necessarily place them in the predator category. The fact that their personality is less than desirable also doesn't say that it is the product or result of earlier abuse, it could mean that they're just unhappy people or a very inconsiderate twit. The second question is asking if you are doing things, whether by choice or directed forced compliance, that are not permitted for God's children. Damaging to one's right relationship with the Heavenly Father. There are certain rules: dos and don'ts for all of God's children to follow whether we agree with them or not. There are reasons, known only to Him, we aren't to challenge His decisions. Examining the aspects of your circumstances and answering yes to either of the questions, you should seek to get out or away from it, tell someone if you're unable to do it without help. Yes, again, you run the risk of that person being more of a hindrance than a help; it doesn't matter...........say something anyway, you just might have misjudged them or they have had a change of heart. God can cause you to find favor with others where there was none before.

Thus far I've mostly addressed the victims of abuse, I will now turn my focus, again, to the person who's life up to this point may be tainted with some sort of unacceptable act, whether it happened just once or multiple times, and now you find that you are more than disgusted with yourself. You're wanting to stop, but you find that that is much harder than you imagined, you're needing help............who can **you** turn to? Who can you trust that won't prejudge you and thereby being ostracized for being honest and sincere?

You, too, have risks of your own even bigger than that of the innocent. I must confess that for many years, after my successful escape from my torture, I only wished harm to befall anyone bringing pain to others. I had no mercy for them, nor did I care what happened to them. God had to show me that the things I harbored in my heart hurt Him, as well as myself. I resisted changing the condition my heart was in for quite awhile, until I came across a little girl. She was about eight years old, but looked like she was only four or five. She was very tiny. I had met her parents as they presented her and her little six year old sister to me in my Sunday school class, they seemed happy and pleased to be parents. The parents, of course, left the room to go to their class, the older girl was sullen and withdrawn, her little sister wanted to have fun, but once she looked toward her older sister for direction or permission to, instead she too, withdrew. I was under the belief, at that moment, that the older girl was a little on the mean and controlling side and sure didn't look like she was going to do any changing any time soon.

I, later, after noticing the girl was secretly watching me, I put the other children to coloring while I tried to strike up a conversation with this girl. She told me that those people were not her parents and did not want to go back with them. Wow, was I ever blown away! She was a tough little girl, she showed no emotion.... none. She did show me that she cared /loved her little sis. My heart melted for her,

I asked where her parents were, but she didn't respond. The bell rang which signaled the end of class and just like that the two were gone. In my heart I was saddened I didn't know what I should or could do, I mean the pair didn't say that they needed or wanted help, and since there was no apparent signs of abuse I had nothing to go on. It wasn't long after that that the girls were shuffled somewhere else and had other caretakers, it was also made known that the people who were caring for them through our church had carried on abusive activity with them. I've, not to my knowledge, not seen them since.

Through this and a couple other incidents the LORD has shown me that, in order for some wanting perpetrators to be able to stop or feel safe turning themselves in, there have to be willing and understanding Godly individuals ready to help them. He showed me that just because I stand with them on their decision of quitting such hurtful and unlawful behavior, did not in any way say that I am protecting them from their consequences nor would it be me upholding said unGodly behavior. It does offer the repentant offender a help in the right direction. In so offering ourselves in that capacity we are not only loving the unlovely but we are being a yielded vessel for God and His wondrous works.

If you are truly repent (sorry) for what you have or are doing God can help you, He's waiting on you,call out to Him and He WILL hear you and answer.

# WHAT WILL PEOPLE THINK OF ME?

## Chapter V

In this day and age we worry about a lot of things; our hair, our clothes, our pay/job, and..."What do people think of me?". We believe that it is a much bigger issue than that of years previous...r-i-g-h-t! Why do we care? Do we draw each breath on the approval or disapproval of others? Can others determine our happiness? We say, "No", but our actions show different.

Well, this is not new, people from every generation since the beginning of man, have cared in some way, how they look and/or are perceived by others. This isn't necessarily a bad thing, unless it becomes the only thing. When we are comparing ourselves to others, we're usually just concentrating on the superficial; what they wear, how much they weigh, what they say, and what they do.

Growing up in a civilization that holds this type of scales of judgment, causes one to believe or only focus on things that are so insignificant in comparison to what is truly important. We do need to look our best, but if "our" best isn't bought at Bloomingdale's or Rodeo Dr., but rather at a thrift store, we need to be happy knowing that we are wearing "our" best. Our happiness should never hinge on someone else or their ideas of what you should wear or do. We tell our children not to pay attention to what other children say or do, and don't worry about what label is on their clothing, they're either your friend or they're not. It is so cut and dried, but we don't follow what we say, my dad used this saying a lot, as I'm certain it is nothing new to your ears either; "do as I say, not as I do". Shouldn't we reclaim that part of us that is free from social peer pressures ?

What we say and do holds a lot of weight with how we are perceived by others. When we are invited to an upscale function, of course we wear our best (hoping it will, at least, pass as suitable), we speak softer and try to use words we don't customarily use in our day to day conversations. That doesn't make us less than or better than another; it just means we are different. We should celebrate our differences and learn from each other.

Knowing these facts changes little. We are so often moved to purchase things that are presented as "cool", or the current fad, giving little heed as to whether it is to our benefit or not. So, is it surprising that our children buckle under the same unsettling pressures, seeing that it has been a part or constant factor in their lives? It shouldn't be.

We hear that the youth of today have it so much worse than those of previous years, but I say, this just isn't true at all! Think about it; the people who lived when the prehistoric beasts roamed the earth had some pretty tough days, I assure you. When the children played outside, I'm sure, they had to be very aware of what was going on around them all of the time. The dangers were ever present, did it keep them hidden inside afraid to come out? No, it didn't. How about the children we read about in the Bible; if they disrespected their elders or were disobedient, they were killed by a bear or other wild animal of that day, OR were stoned to death. Some, were used as a sacrificial offering to appease different gods. Let's look at the children from any of the hundreds, if not thousands, of wars in history, they had to "grow up" real quick; dodging bullets and scraping for anything of value to exchange for food. Some became orphans and homeless in less than a wink, while others had to take care of the rest of their families by any means possible. Learning what it took to survive and help their families in these "life and death" situations. Not knowing what would happen to them, whether they would live or die, from one moment to the next; much less if they were going to eat. They faced the blunt realities of war, death, destruction, poverty, and uncertainty, everyday during the harshest of times. Even in their unfathomable situations, they still found something to press toward, something that caused them to smile/laugh again. And finally, children of the wars and devastation of our lifetime. We are shown children of other countries living in war zones, starving, wearing little more than rags. Their eyes tell you they're suffering, the narrator keeps driving home the idea, "we need to help these that can't help themselves, the innocent victims", we quickly give aid and readily spout our good deed(s) for all to hear and know that we are "good", because we came to their rescue.

We are so caught up and consumed by our self worth, that we turn a blind eye and deaf ear to the harsh realities within our own country, states, communities, and homes. Everyday a innumerable measure of people, of all ages, are suffering in many ways. Some are hungry, unhappy, lonely, dissatisfied with how their life is going, and the list goes on and on; but, I know, there is a great number who are victims of hate crimes, verbal and/or physical abuse, sexual assault, and rape. Even though rape is most generally considerate a type of sexual assault, many states have varying definitions of the two; so, I too, will divide them, for their sakes.

Reaching out to someone can be scary in itself, not knowing who you can trust, Will they believe me? Are they friends with or related to the abuser? And how will they handle this…………, the questions and fears go on and on. In my own life I battled with these same haunting questions. I had even plotted suicide as a way out of the torturous life I was having to live, but there was something inside of me that said, "do not let these people and their actions take your life, I love you!" Even though it has been thirty-eight years ago, I remember that evening as if it were yesterday, I knew that no one else was in the room with me to speak those words, as I also knew that it wasn't me either, because I felt worthless at that point. Who was it? Then, I didn't know, but, today, I know without doubt or hesitation that it was the Holy Spirit speaking to me, ministering to me, just what I needed!

In public, people would/will tell you I was a happy child, I lived life to the fullest, loved all those around me; even my enemies, and laughed everyday of my life; but within the confines of my caretakers, it was as different as night and day! I was not permitted to visit others alone, it didn't matter whether they were children or adults, or get to stay over at my friend's houses, and they were not going to get to stay with me at my house, either! I was not allowed to attend parties of any kind, and at school I was very forcibly reminded, "not to get close to any adult", if I did, they would know about it and certain bad things would happen to those persons. When I was older, and I had been successful at getting the sexual assaults/rapes to end by placing my very breath on the line, I was still denied permission to get a job, where I could possibly share my story and thus a spotlight of that knowledge would reveal the ugliness of my caretakers actions on/ against me; thereby, holding them accountable in a court of law.

Shouldn't we wonder why: if we love our families and neighbors as we're suppose to (as Christ loves us [the church] ), we offer support of every kind, and we provide their needs/wants; how is it then, that there isn't enough assurance in their relationship with us? What can, or who can, hold such power or control over them that their confidence in us begins to wane?

No earthly being can know the heart or mind of another. We might think we know, or hope we know, but when it comes right down to it we have to face facts; as long as "man" has a mind and freedom of thought we will not be able to figure each others total response. I recall a certain popular television program that was on in the eighties, that took parent's of young children aside, they would ask them what they thought their youngster would do in certain situations, like helping a stranger find a supposed lost puppy. Of course, each parent had believed that they had instilled enough knowledge to not be taken in by these traps, and/or made them aware of the ever present danger in speaking with a strange adult. Up for the challenge they sat with confidence in an area just out of sight from their child, watching the scene unfold on a monitor. A man; clean cut, well dressed, and mild mannered, and of course working with the film crew, approached the child. He didn't just rush over, not wanting to alarm the child. He said, "hi", but acted as if that wasn't his main focus, he let the child think he was just there. The child was relaxed and didn't appear frightened in any way. Then, the man asked calmly, "have you seen a puppy running around here? I was out here playing with it and it ran this way, I just thought you might have seen it." acting as if he was going to walk on, then briefly hesitating he added,"well, I'll keep looking for it........ would you help me?"

The person that sat hidden from the child's view with the mother, turned and asked, "do you think they'll go with him?" She quickly said that they had practiced this same scenario and she felt satisfied that the child would remember the lesson and refuse to help the man. Sitting and waiting she witnessed a horrifying sight, her child not only went with the stranger, but the stranger was able to put his hand on the small child's shoulder. The fact that the child allowed the stranger to put his hand on his person probably doesn't mean a whole lot, but to a parent, potential perpetrator, or to a former abuse victim it signifies that the child has completely let his/her guard down leaving themselves wide open for a myriad troubles / abuse.

These scenes unfold time after time day after day, we can only pray that our loved ones not be among the victimized. We have to push forward keeping a watchful eye on all that concerns us, but most of all keep the lines of communication open between us and God, He will bring us through it all! It may not always make sense to us, but He knows the beginning and the end of all things. We just need to trust Him and believe that He will do what is best for us or on our behalf. What others may or may not

# WHY DID GOD DO THIS....
# I THOUGHT HE LOVED ME?

## Chapter VI

There is nowhere you can go these days that you don't hear, at least once, "Why has God done/caused this....?" Repeatedly, it is said by the Christians as often as the non-Christians. I have tried to help people understand that God loves us and only wants the best for us, but we cannot over look the fact that things will happen for various reasons. Yes, it is true satan has a good hold on this Earth and a big part of it's inhabitants, but God hasn't abdicated His throne, He is well aware of everyone and every movement.

Even in our God given manual there are many times that our predecessors have had the same thoughts and feelings; wondering, "if God is love......why do we suffer so?" It is said that we suffer because we are alive and that that is just a normal part of life. Where God comes into the picture is when faith is exercised. There various accounts throughout the pages where something or someone needed or wanted something to happen or not, and the prayers or needs seemed to be ignored or fall upon deaf ears, but it was due to a lack or the absence of faith on the part of those seeking help.

I am not, in any way, trying to say that I've never been confused or stressed out passing understanding, that would not be so; there have been many occasions that I have searched my mind to exhaustion trying to figure out why this or that has happened, or why it is going to happen. I am reminded each time, that we can't know everything that concerns another person(s) mind nor intentions, but God says that we can turn everything over to Him and He will take care of us and all that concerns us.

The main reason we are not experiencing these "answered prayers/requests" is largely do to: we find it difficult to turn anything over to anyone because we want to be in complete control, even if we have no idea how to handle it. The very idea that we relinquish our hold on anything is absurd. We people, as a whole, like to be "in control"; I believe that it is a vital part of who we are. We are expected to "step up" as a batter does to the plate to take our turn, but, unlike the batter, we are not standing alone; yes, there are the people behind the batter shouting and cheering them on, but they are only spectators, they're not there to help you perform past that of encouragement from a distance, they sit in the stands watching you perform your task(s) at hand, offering their bits of suggestions on how you could do better. You have, I'm sure, heard people say; "I know just how you feel", but do they? No matter, God does and HE is waiting to help you!

When we encounter something in our day that gets our undivided attention we need to realize that – 1. Things happen and no matter how long we live they will continue to happen, until we draw our last breath. And - 2. It is nothing new, someone has been through this before, you may have never been through it or had it happen to you before, but someone has. God is never shocked nor taken off guard, He is merely waiting on us to yield to His will.

God isn't ignorant to our circumstances either, He gives us all freedom of choice and what happens as a result of those choices is already been made available to us in His book; both good and bad, we need to read it so we can know it and thereby live by it.

I'm not pretending that life is easy once you profess your belief in God or your wanting Him to heal or answer you on certain things. No, quite the contrary, it is usually harder. We are taught that once God comes into the picture all is good, kind and fair; wrong! We still need to be alert for traps, snares,and or temptations. God is our help, but we still need to be working and looking for ways to live according to His purpose for our lives.

The days of trouble can come upon anyone at any given time. We, like I have already stated, can't know the mind nor intentions of another, and not forgetting; that God has given us all freedom to choose to do/be good or not, but......if we are aware of our surroundings the likelihood of certain crimes is lessened. Other more sinister crimes are so undetectable that there really is no way of protecting ourselves in advance. Looking to God before, during, and after such an offense can be the only thing that saves us. I was pretty young when my first trouble came upon me, I was too little to fully comprehend the whole scope of God, His Son, and the Holy Spirit. I knew nothing actually, I was only a toddler. I remember a person always being around. He had a kind face, I was never afraid of him. He never spoke out loud to me, but I knew he was there to help me. Once when I was five years old I was up before daylight, I was walking down the stairs in my house when I saw the man again, we exchanged our usual smiles but never spoke, I was not afraid. The next morning I relayed the sighting to one of my caretakers, as I spoke I watched her face change from a soft pretty face to one that was harsh and angry. I was surprised, I thought that this would please her, but it didn't. Years later I was invited to a Sunday school class, I was about 20 by this time. When I walked into the class I came face to face with the man I had seen throughout my childhood, it was a picture hanging on the front wall of this room. I now knew that Jesus had been my helper all of those years, even though I didn't know Him He knew me.

Having spent many years counseling people of all ages and backgrounds and seeing the devastation of abuse in about every form you could imagine, both in the church as well as outside the church walls. Each victim telling, sharing, relaying their story as if it had just taken place. The fear shown on their faces as if it were the same. After letting them clear themselves of what they wanted to say I'd ask a series of questions upon which they would answer. One of my questions would always be, "Why do you suppose this has happened to you?", in almost every instance I hear them say, "this is God's will, I'm suppose to learn something from it." WHAT!!!! It is all I can do to sit there and let them continue, but I do I don't want them to feel threatened in anyway, I realize that they were taught wrong and they have not researched it for themselves.

When I was teaching a Sunday school class of seven to nine year old's I was trying to get them to understand something too few people do, so, I wrote on the chalk board a "scripture" that read, "It is a sin to chew bubble gum. I Peter 3:8" then I waited for them to arrive. One by one they filed into class, there were six or seven as I remember. They had taken a seat and quietly waited on their straggling friends, soon we would open with a short prayer. I begin to pick up on some low whispers, it was so cute watching their little sleepy faces come alive upon reading the board. Finally one brave soul raised his hand and asked if it were true.

I wanted a bit more interaction from them so I asked to what was he referring to, he pointed at the writing on the board, that! Is it true, is it a sin to chew gum?! Before I could respond the rest of the sleepy heads snapped to attention as if on cue. Well, what have I always told you? Their faces were filled with puzzled looks. LOOK IT UP!!!! The books were opened faster than any at a Bible drill, they zipped through those pages just as fast. It was thrilling to see them so keen on finding an answer.

"Hey, it doesn't say that!" a boy said so confidently, with others chiming in.

"It doesn't?" I asked.

"No, you lied to us."

"No, I'm teaching you all a very good lesson, no matter where, what, or who tells you anything.........check......it....... out!!!" I know some will not understand this, some may not like it, I can't help that I teach what I teach to try and help others, so they can't or won't fall prey to a lot of wrong teaching.

I'd like to believe that these little ones grew up and went out into their chosen paths, taking with them these nuggets of wisdom and teaching. I'd like to also believe that none of them ever suffered failure, lost a job, ever went through times where they were alone or just felt like no one cared for them. The decisions they've made have always been good Godly ones. Their relationships throughout with God and man have been close and right.

And finally, that none of them nor their offspring have suffered at the hands of another in any wrongful way that would have them living with hurt and hate.

The thought that this is true would be a utopia. The fact is: people make mistakes, wrong choices, lie, cheat, steal, leave God, cuss God, blame God, accuse God, they get hurt and cause hurt and death, finally; people realize that this world is a tough place to live, BUT it is when we hold tight to God, trust Him always no matter what we have gone through or are experiencing now, He will help us! HE LOVES US ALL, we have to choose Him, He is not rude nor pushy, He doesn't demand you to do this or that, but if you are wanting Him to be your help and guide, then allow Him to lead and do exactly what He says or requires. He has promised that HE WILL NEVER leave us or forsake us! He loves us!

# SHOULD I HATE THE PERPETRATOR?

## Chapter VII

Realizing that you have, or are, suffering at the hands or intentions of another, it would be understandable, if not expected that "hate" would be a major factor in your life from there on out. I, myself, had to deal with that ugly part of being a victim. I would seclude myself off from everyone, I had nothing to say and I sure had nothing I wanted to hear. I spent a good five to eight years hating many things: me, the ones holding me captive, my caregivers, the people I tried to get help from, the list goes on and on............

Living that way made me a very bitter person, yes, I appeared happy on the outside so I'd be left alone, but on the inside was a raging hatred wanting to explode on everything and everyone. I was so full of hate I kept all future relationship hopefuls of any kind away. I never cried, not at funerals, getting cut pretty badly, not over sad movies, not even watching one of my caregivers getting their stomach pumped after ingesting a bottle of pills to end their life and a code blue was called, nothing brought me to tears. I did not cry because I was through spilling tears and not being heard.

I noticed that my missing a meal seemed to capture more attention than my being repeatedly victimized, that is when I decided to take control of me, no one else could control my eating; they might control the rest of my life and death, but not that. I wouldn't eat for days, then it was easy,

I'd go weeks. I felt great, I finally had a sense of power over me. I worked two full time jobs while still depriving my body of food and sleep. I was getting everyone's full attention now. They were calling one to another checking to see when and where and possibly what I had eaten, the only thing anyone could report was,"Nothing"! I WAS IN CONTROL!!!

I began feeling differently, with this sense of control came self confidence, I was actually looking forward to the day. I began making new friends, I bought myself new clothes that fit! I took this co-worker up on an invite to Resurrection Sunday, I enjoyed the place, the sermon and the people. I felt like I belonged. I continued to attend that church on a regular basis even when my co-worker/friend didn't. I enjoyed the beautiful music, the smiling faces and the overall feel of the place.

My friend had spoken to me on numerous occasions about my not eating, I understood her concern...but I was in control. She worried about it being the death of me, I assured her that I had it all under control. I also cautioned her about talking to anyone about it. One afternoon, we went to the church as usual, this time we sat toward the back, the place was full. The minister's first words were,"I don't know who this is for, but "starving yourself is a sin". I was horrified, I just knew that my friend had said something to him, so I took a hand to her face. She insisted that she had said nothing, she told me that that is how God speaks to us sometimes. I was furious with her, how could she betray me.....I trusted her!

Days passed I didn't know what to make of the whole thing, but if I was committing a sin by not eating I should stop......how? I had done this for so long I didn't know how to quit. I learned how to pray, I started asking God for help, one evening I went to my friend's house, she'd quit asking if I wanted any food awhile earlier, I asked her what they had had for supper. Beef and noodles she replied.

Do you have any left I asked. I thought she was going to leap on me, she was so excited. I was apprehensive at first, but I thought of other things like you would normally do when you eat. I ate the whole bowl! I was elated and thankful. Years later I found out that because of the abuse I had done to my body my body has protected itself against being deprived of food again, it stores everything. I suffer now because of a little word called "hate" that I harbored and fed and allowed to grow inside of me, even though I am a Christian and God had healed me of this eating disorder I had been forgiven of this sin, I still have to live with the consequences of my past choices.

Hate is ugly, it causes sickness and disease even after the initial hate is gone. We are to pray for and love one another, hating only the sin that they commit. Get away from the abuser, don't think that God finds joy in that suffering, He doesn't.

Upon hearing these words many have thoughts and/ or suggestions on how they would deal with someone who has done these wicked vile acts against another. Hearing them describe their detailed accounts of "the cure", everything from rotting in prison to ridding them of some body parts; makes me wonder why they think that their way of thinking is correct against that of the criminal. Yes,I was and am still angry that these atrocities go on day after day. I once interviewed a practicing psychiatrist for my studies on human behavior. I asked him several questions, nothing too far different than anyone else would have, but then, he added to one of the answers he'd just given; "there is nothing that you can think of or try to contrive in your wildest imagination that hasn't been done or is going on right this very second."

Just hearing him utter that statement sent a eerie chill down my spine. I have heard it said that there is nothing new under the sun, but I imagined that to pertain to inventions and such not evil doings as well. When I left his office I thought back over the whole session, but I couldn't help replaying his statement about our not being able to come up with something good or bad, to whatever degree, that someone hasn't thought of and done already. God forgive our wickedness! I say, "our" because if it weren't for God's grace where would anyone of us be, or what would we be guilty of?

I decided long ago after hearing another Sunday school teacher say, "Has anyone in this class ever hated someone?" My mind quickly rummaged through my files, (in my head I keep my thoughts and things in a filing cabinet and every time I need to recall something I visualize opening it up, as one would in the physical to retrieve the needed information.) I pulled several files that would have easily fit in the category of hate for one reason or another, but there was one that seem to stand out more than the others. Yes, this person had been so mean and wicked to me for many years and was still inflicting their wickedness on me. The teacher went on, "If you hate another person, whether for a just cause or not, you will become like this person.)

The class was in shock, you could hear gasps from us all. I knew she had to be wrong, I was nothing like this wicked person who hurts me so badly! I really don't know what else was said that day in class, my mind was too busy trying to figure this horrifying statement out. All the way home I thought about it, I thought she surely is wrong, I'm not guilty of hurting others. I've not done these hideous things! How am I like them?!

I, also can't recall how many hours I spent in deep thought over this subject, but it was many! Then, I let my mind rest after reaching an exhausted state. Quietly I laid on bed, letting my whole body relax especially my mind. After what seemed like hours, which might have only been minutes, I began forming thoughts that were like whispering conversations. No, I wasn't losing my mind. This was just a very still moment. The gist of the conversation or as I would later understand, the reasons for....., was: When we harbour hate, bitterness, and hurts we are allowing them to attack us from the inside, where they root themselves and become a rotting detestable spirit. Leaving ourselves wide open for ill feelings and feelings of believed righteous retaliation. Behaving in a way we would have not normally done, causing hurt and pain to others even those who are trying to help. All the while changing from a reasonably good and healthy person who'd been victimized to this almost inhuman beast. So, understanding this transformation and how it began as a hurt and became hate, watching it take on a life of it's own, one can see that not recognizing the importance of ridding ourselves of these bad unwanted attachments can turn us into the very thing that hurt us in the first place. We would become as vile as the one who originally hurt us. Maybe the hurts or people aren't the same, but the results are! I am NOT in any way offering

# HOW DO I FORGIVE SOMEONE WHO DOESN'T BELIEVE THAT THEY'VE DONE ANYTHING WRONG?

## Chapter VIII

Part of the healing process is either, hearing that the person is remorseful and is hoping for some sort of mercy; or you could, at least, believe that they were sorry. Having this, you are fully able to step forward from the ashes of this indescribable situation or place into the rest of your life.

I know what it is to suffer grievously, over a long period time (years), at the hands of the very people that were to keep me FROM harm! Again, to everyone else, it seemed that I was happy and healthy, that couldn't be further from the truth.

You may be wondering why I was so long in this anguish, why I never acted anything other than happy. If I had acted distressed, sad, mad, and/or even lonely, someone might have come to my rescue. Well, as I have explained in previous chapters, and if you have been unfortunate to experience anything similar, you already know; it can vary from simple threats against you, to threats against the well being of your family and friends, and finally, depending on the circumstances, it is embarrassing to have others know; you have gotten yourself in this situation. Of course, the latter is totally a figment of our imagination or one invented by our captor/abuser to insure further secrecy.

Sometimes, the question is,"should I or do I have to forgive the perpetrator?" I have found in my own life and experiences, that hanging on to bitterness, anger, blame, or even hurt; I limit myself only. I realized many years after getting away, that, until I find a way to get these questions and awful visuals out of my brain, I would have no peace. I had no idea how to do this.

I had always felt drawn to church, I couldn't understand why I seemed to be the only one out of this large number of people (13) in the house that had this need to go. I would get up very early and quietly get myself around. I don't remember my feeling it necessary to get permission, I just did it. I would wait on the big front porch for whatever church bus that happened by. I ended up going to nearly every church in town with the exception of two, and that's just because they didn't have a bus. I had invited the other persons in the house, I had even gotten four of the younger ones ready on several occasions, but that was stopped because their parents said they didn't want their children forced to go. Soon after three more persons were added to the residence, but sadly, they too declined my invitations.

Well, the years passed as they do, I continued my church bus hopping even into my teens and no matter what house or new town I was shuffled off to. I really don't or can't say that this fact from my early years did much in the way of receiving great and monumental revelations, but it did seem to give me an unchanging place of solidity. I always felt"at home" wherever I entered His house.

I have told you these things to assure you that even though the vulgar unspeakable things were done to me,

I longed for Sundays! I, too, had to hear the boastings and laughter most have felt, when the evil ones have felt justified. I was often made to feel like dirt, that I wasn't worth words. The one who held me captive looked and acted like a saint. Meanwhile all those who "knew" him rallied around him like he was one as well. I even found myself hating them worse than the one who was to blame. How could they be so blind?!!!

No matter how hard I tried to show or tell this person just how wrong this was, the more they pointed out that it was their "duty", showing me just how cruel people can be, getting me prepared to be a true adult in this wicked world. He felt fully vindicated. There is no way to deal with a person who fully believes that they are doing good, even when what they are doing is completely insane.

There is no easy fix for this! We have to find our answers and help in getting ourselves right, never compromising on what is right and Holy. Keep wisdom and love close and maintain a healthy relationship with our Heavenly Father. He sees and knows everything that we have and are going through, but mostly, He knows who did these things AND HE will repay them on our behalf.

I must add:while it is hard to believe that they can receive forgiveness just like you or I, we must not dwell on them we have to move on for our own sanity and wellness. Besides, we aren't even forgiven until we recognize our need for it and seek God's mercy and grace AND we turn from that thing that has found us outside of His will. I have heard people misquote scripture fitting it to their way of thinking or their desires for one reason or another; the way I understand it: we are to forgive the ones who ask for it, but not until then, and we are to carry on as if that past offense isn't masking your inward feeling of acceptance of them We do not have to go back to the way things were before the offense. Each instance is different in what has happened to the severity of hurt, but the same steps apply.

I used to dream of how I was going to punish the person(s) that hurt me, every part was carefully planned. Everything from public humiliation to bodily harm, even to the taking of their life. I became almost possessed with these thoughts, that in doing these things I would make them suffer like I did, make them pay for what they had done to me, and finally, to let all of their followers see just how wicked they were. Then, one day God showed me just how I had become so consumed with paying them back that I was now in need of His forgiveness and restoration.

Hearing this in my soul was so outrageous, but it was true! I let God lead and I followed, He healed me. Today I am clear of that desire and am satisfied I will never have it return, if it tries, God will handle it!

# TRANSFORMATION

Knowing that abuse is never okay, in any form or severity, one should never tolerate it! It won't stop until something or someone intervenes. One should be aware that the circumstances or situation, most likely, wasn't their fault. You can't know in everyday life that one person or another is going to attack you. Oh, sometimes you might be alerted by a way a person is acting, as in following too close or watching you as you shop or go about your usual manner. In some cases a person has taken an unusual interest in you or your children. These people should be watched closely and never let your guard down. This isn't to say that every kind person who speaks to you is a suspected violent criminal. We have got to put safety measures in balance or we might just miss some really great opportunities God has for us.

We have got to learn how to rid ourselves of the fears, anger, hurts, bitterness etc........ These are weights around our necks and sinkers to our souls. We believe that they are hidden out of sight to the others we come into contact with, and that we have them under our control. That is where self-deception comes in, we are the only ones that can't see their effects, maybe we are in denial.

When I say, "we", I am not only talking about you and others out there who have or are trying to deal with the hideous residue left behind, but I am including myself. I believed, that when I had gotten rid of or stopped the abuse in my life that it was over! Now, I could live a "NORMAL" life, like everybody else, much to my surprise, I was not the person I once was. The people around me made comments to that effect. I found myself staying to myself, I wasn't rude, I was still the seemingly happy person..... on the outside, but a storm was brewing on the inside. I sat quietly for long periods of time thinking about all sorts of things. I would not realize that people were actually speaking to me, until they would either repeat themselves several times (I was told after I snapped back to reality) or by them touching my arm to get my attention. By their laughter I could see this isn't that normal. I found myself almost hating people with an arrogant domineering presence, most like that of my abusers. When I had no choices nor control over what I said or did, these instances would take me back mentally to that horrible part of my life. One time that stands out more than any other; I had been away from my abusive past for about four years when I had been summoned by my peers to meet the new person. I could hear her boisterous laugh even before I had gotten to the doorway, I could hear her voice; it grated on my very last nerve I felt a defense wall going up deep inside of myself, I wanted to turn and go the other way rather than meeting her, but, as to appear, "normal" I entered the room where we were to meet, along with everyone else. She and I were about the same age I figured, I learned later that she was a year older than me. The manner in which she presented herself, her fashion of dress, and even her mannerisms themselves showed her to be impertinent. It was very evident that her and I clashed, it had nothing to do with our personalities, she appeared happy and bubbly, by all accounts we should have clicked.

The fact was, as I was to discover years later, she hadn't done anything to me except resemble someone I thought I was finished with. A person who had controlled my very breath, and at that time there was nothing that I could do but hope that help would come....none did, leaving me (at that time) feeling helpless, worthless and alone. So, when this attitude presented itself right in my comfort zone, causing me to feel angst and a feeling of never being completely free from it. I, like anyone, felt (though subconsciously) I should protect myself, I never let her in to my "real me" and she knew it.

I carried those weights and woes around on the inside for many years until a friend of mine invited me to a "singspiration", while I enjoyed the beautiful music I felt a drawing toward this place, I couldn't explain it. I had been in and out of churches up to that point I had never felt that way before. I wanted to check this out further, so I continued going even when my friend didn't. I felt such an unexplainable but welcomed peace whenever I'd enter the doors of that church. I listened intently to the words that the preacher spoke, I watched the other people around me, this was so wonderful to me. Before I realized it I had been going for several months, my family, friends, and co-workers were confused; they wondered why I continued to go where none of them were at. I invited them to the next service, but they, for some reason or another, couldn't make it. They'd invite me to their functions and festivities, but I didn't want to miss what the preacher had to say, so I'd politely decline.

I heard that God was everywhere and that He loved us; now, I had already learned that He loved us but that He was everywhere, that was new to me. Weeks and months passed I learned that God heals, He never meant for us to suffer and die, but because sin had entered in to His perfect place we will suffer and die. He sent His Son Jesus to be our Saviour, the Saviour of this whole wide world, Jesus took sickness and disease and the sins of us all to the cross. He did it willingly and with much love, even though we don't deserve it. I heard all of these things, I wanted to be free from the ugliness of my past. During one of the services when I was twenty-four I stepped out and away from my pew and began that walk to the front. Others were walking as well, at the front the preacher asked the remainder of the congregats to come along behind us to join in prayer. Each person shared their request(s) with him as he came to them, after telling him their wants or needs we'd all pray for that individual. Then, it was my turn I began to be fearful, maybe I didn't understand, maybe I wasn't doing this right, what would I ask for?

"What would you have the Lord do for you?" I heard, along, with the beating of my heart.

I looked at the preacher and the crowd around me, everyone was starring, waiting to hear my request so they could join me in prayer. It seemed like a scene from a movie, all my focus was on my heart which sounded like beating war drums from an old western. "Well, sir" I could hear myself say, "I would like a new heart!" I finished with a boldness not known to me before.

Right there and then the whole group began to pray, I bowed my head in reverence I really didn't know what to do or say. The preacher said to me while the people continued their praying, "just know that He is able and willing to do all and anything we ask in Jesus' name. Just talk to Him, He is listening, He knows your every hurt and care."

I knew from that night on God gave me a new heart, it had to happen my old one was broken and scarred, it had become hard and callused, it was full of grief and hatred; I knew I needed a heart "non-surgical transplant", only God could do that. I had people coming up to me then and even to this day saying that my laughter is joyous and my face glows with His presence.

I don't know what you have gone through or are suffering with at this very moment in your life, but there is help and hope. God is still on the throne and is very aware of your situation, He cares for you more than you could ever understand much less try to measure. He knows the condition as well as the intentions of your heart and the very thoughts of your mind, all He requires: believe that He is, and that He had a son named Jesus whom He freely gave as the ultimate sacrifice, and that through Him is how you approach the Father, no other way, and do not offend His Holy Ghost (Spirit). Once you have decided to follow Him, He will direct your your steps, though many times you'll mess up, that's when you pick yourself up, dust yourself off and continue on. There will be many times you will feel alone as you walk, but you won't be, He will be right there with you no matter what you are going through, good or bad.

My attention now will shift to anyone that might have come across this book in a way you just can't explain or understand. It was no accident, God put this book in your hands just as surely as you are breathing. You might have committed an act of abuse or violence against another individual(s), whether you meant to or not someone has suffered as result.

I, myself being a survivor, can see where you, as an abuser or former violent person would be slightly apprehensive to seek help for your problem or disorder. I can equally understand other survivors or family members of the victims who didn't survive, not be willing to forgive and forget. I had to overcome those feelings before I could move forward with my own life. Forgiving the people who had hurt me was the one thing I never wasted any time or energy on, as far as I was concerned I didn't care what happened to them, I was just thankful to escape. I learned in the years following that God does care for them as much as He cares and loves me. I, at first, was angry about that, how could God love the very person that had done such horrible things to me and caused me so much pain?! This just couldn't be, that to me was adding insult to injury.

I put it out of my mind and tried to live on, as normal a life as one could. I got a job, then another, and at nineteen I had two full time jobs and still felt like I needed to do more. I filled my days so full that the only things running through my mind were the responsibilities associated with the jobs I was working. I was likened to a workaholic which, at that time, I took as a compliment, later I realized it wasn't.

I have spent many hours, days, weeks..........years changing people's perception of life. Showing them, no matter which side of the equation they're on, they need to see it through the eyes of God our Father. I am actually excited when I am given an opportunity to reach another victim or another perpetrator. They have come to me for counseling, they're broken and have no idea what to do or where to go, they're tired of living their life as it is they are ready for something to change. I begin, of course, since I am a Christian and would not want to see anyone die and go to a place that was originally created for satan and all who followed him, I find out where they are spiritually. Some have never heard or know about Christ Jesus, others have been brought up in the church and still never knew Him, then there are those who were once traveling on the right course in life and for one reason or another sidestepped, doing things that does not glorify our Heavenly Father. After establishing there spiritual status then I move on to evaluating their current mental state, only then can I turn my attention or focus on why they think they have come in.

No matter, where you are at on your road to recovery or whichever side of the equation you find yourself on always remember that God can do anything! He can take the hurting, the wounded and heal them completely. He can take the vilest sinner and make them whiter than snow. Transforming them both into forgiven loved members of society, bringing them through many trials and troubles, making us all ready for Him!

# LETTER TO THE READER

Having read all of the contents of this writing and if you have gleaned even the smallest of help, then my purpose for writing this has done its job.

I'm not claiming to have all of the answers, I'm merely trying to offer some insight into both the victim and the perpetrator's minds. While, at the same time helping the rest of the world know what is, most commonly, running through the mind and heart of them both.

I'm even writing to the person(s) who are already or are about to be offering help to these people. it is a long hard process to bring forth health to the body and mind. Sometimes it seems hopeless and maybe that person isn't ready to be helped, if that is so don't stop helping, others are ready! God be with you!

# ABOUT THE AUTHOR

Like all of you, I was born. The specifics ie; place of birth, names of parents, race, or ages etc., are not important.

Very early in my life I became a victim of abuse, it came in various forms. Being very young when it began I never even thought about it not being normal. It never occurred to me that it was wrong, to me it was my life, there was no way for me to know any different.

Later, when I was about nine or ten, I was shocked to learn; this is not normal, not everyone goes through this. My life changed drastically that day! Even though I was still being abused I knew in my mind that this should not be happening and it needs to stop! I, from that day on, began plotting a way for that to happen, how and when, I did not know, but I wasn't going to give up until then.

I did escape the abuse only to have it come back to me through the gut wrenching stories of the many people, both young and old, that I have counseled over these almost forty years.

I have made it my business to be about doing God's business. I am very busy counseling and encouraging hurt and damaged lives get to the one that can bring them from being a victim to being VICTORIOUS with God!